THE BUSINESS OF LISTENING

A Practical Guide to Effective Listening

REVISED EDITION

Diane Bone

A FIFTY-MINUTE™ SERIES BOOK

CRISP PUBLICATIONS, INC.
Menlo Park, California

THE BUSINESS OF LISTENING

A Practical Guide to Effective Listening

REVISED EDITION

Diane Bone

CREDITS
Editor: **Michael Crisp**
Layout & Composition: **Interface Studio**
Cover Design: **Carol Harris**
Artwork: **Ralph Mapson**

Copyright © 1988, 1994 by Crisp Publications, Inc.
Printed in the United States of America

English language Crisp books are distributed worldwide. Our major international distributors include:

CANADA: Reid Publishing, Ltd., Box 69559—109 Thomas St., Oakville, Ontario Canada L6J 7R4. TEL: (416) 842-4428, FAX: (416) 842-9327

AUSTRALIA: Career Builders, P. O. Box 1051, Springwood, Brisbane, Queensland, Australia 4127. TEL: 841-1061, FAX: 841-1580

NEW ZEALAND: Career Builders, P. O. Box 571, Manurewa, Auckland, New Zealand. TEL: 266-5276, FAX: 266-4152

JAPAN: Phoenix Associates Co., Mizuho Bldg. 2-12-2, Kami Osaki, Shinagawa-Ku, Tokyo 141, Japan. TEL: 3-443-7231, FAX: 3-443-7640

Selected Crisp titles are also available in other languages. Contact International Rights Manager Suzanne Kelly at (415) 323-6100 for more information.

Library of Congress Catalog Card Number 93-74408
Bone, Diane
The Business of Listening
ISBN 1-56052-286-0

This book is printed on recyclable paper with soy ink.

ABOUT THIS BOOK

THE BUSINESS OF LISTENING is not like most books. It stands out from other self-help books in an important way. It's not a book to read—it's a book to *use*. The unique "self-paced" format of this book and the many worksheets, encourage the reader to get involved and, try some new ideas immediately.

Using the simple yet sound techniques presented can make a dramatic change in one's ability to listen effectively.

THE BUSINESS OF LISTENING can be used effectively in a number of ways. Here are some possibilities:

—**Individual Study.** Because the book is self-instructional, all that is needed is a quiet place, some time and a pencil. By completing the activities and exercises, a reader should not only receive valuable feedback, but also practical steps for self-improvement.

—**Workshops and Seminars.** The book is ideal for assigned reading prior to a workshop or seminar. With the basics in hand, the quality of the participation will improve, and more time can be spent on concept extensions and applications during the program. The book is also effective when it is distributed at the beginning of a session, and participants "work through" the contents.

—**Remote Location Training.** Books can be sent to those not able to attend "home office" training sessions.

There are several other possibilities that depend on the objectives, program or ideas of the user.

One thing for sure, even after it has been read, this book will be looked at—and thought about—again and again.

DEDICATION

This book is dedicated to my husband, Gary Romero, who has shown me that being a good listener is easier than living with one.

Diana Bonet

PREFACE

If you want to improve your ability to listen effectively in your business and personal life, this book is for you. Most of us are not good listeners. While at work, we normally listen at about 25 percent of our listening capacity. Most of us *think* we are good listeners, and that overconfidence may be the reason for our downfall. Even if we devote full concentration to listening we cannot listen at 100 percent efficiency for very long. And at 100 percent efficiency, the message we are listening to must be urgent to sustain our attention.

Aside from breathing, humans listen more than anything. Carefully reading this book will help you learn to listen better, on the job and at home. Before good listening can happen you must *want* to be a good listener. Whether you are a secretary, an account executive, a programmer or a project manager, you can improve your listening if you have the desire, the interest, a high level of concentration, self-discipline and a positive attitude.

This book will provide you with important listening know-how. It is a self-study introduction to the basic skills you need to become a better listener. It provides many helpful suggestions for incorporating more effective listening skills into your business day. However, listening styles and motivation are highly individual, so there is no claim as to how much your listening skills will improve. We offer many suggestions for improvement, along with some motivation to help you make constructive changes in your listening style. After completing THE BUSINESS OF LISTENING, you can practice your new-found listening awareness on business associates, family and friends.

Each section in this book provides insightful information, useful tips and practical guidelines for upgrading your skills. These are the *why, what* and *how* of listening. Each section contains activities called "Listening Labs" as well as case studies and check lists. They provide "hands on" reinforcements and illustrations for the key principles of the book.

Part I provides answers to the important question, "Why should I become a better listener?"

Part II describes how good listeners process information and reach higher levels of listening expertise.

Part III identifies individual listening styles as barriers or bridges to communication.

Part IV contains pencil exercises to help you define your listening strengths and weaknesses.

Part V provides ten tips to reinforce your listening strengths, control your weaknesses and reach new levels of listening effectiveness.

Plan to find three ideas from this book to begin practicing immediately. Use *The Business of Listening* as a reference and challenge yourself to practice until you have mastered each new skill. Remember: practice does not make perfect, it makes permanent. Listening well will help you function more effectively in both your business *and* personal life. So pick up your pencil, tune up your ears and turn to Section I.

Happy Listening!

Diane Bone

Diane Bone

SOME IMPORTANT OBJECTIVES FOR THE READER

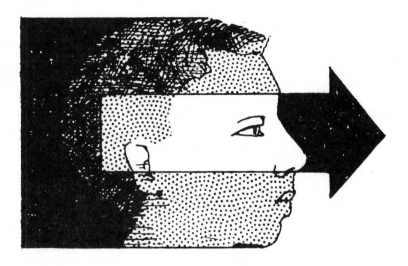

Objectives give us a sense of direction; a definition of what we plan to accomplish; and a sense of fulfillment when they are achieved. Check the objectives that are important to you. This book will help you achieve them.

By completing this book, I plan to:

☐ Learn the basics of effective listening skills.

☐ Learn to recognize good listening behaviors and incorporate them into my daily activities.

☐ Understand the impact of good listening skills on productivity.

☑ Learn to correct problems caused by poor listening habits and systematically change them into permanent good habits.

CONTENTS

Preface   ii
Some Important Objectives for the Reader   v
The Business of Listening   viii

PART I   Why Should You Listen?   1
What's In It For Me?   3
Why Should We Listen?   10
The Joy of Small Change   13

PART II   Four Key Elements of Good Listening   15
How to Be a Good Listener   17
Key Element #1   Hear the Message   20
Key Element #2   Interpret the Message   24
Key Element #3   Evaluate the Message   27
Key Element #4   Respond to the Message   29
Review Lab for Key Elements 1–4   31

PART III   Your Listening Style: A Barrier or A Bridge?   33
Barriers to Communication   35
Bridges to Communication   38

PART IV   How Well Do You Listen?   41
A Listening Attitude: Your Key to Success   43
Personal Listening Inventory   46
How to Stomp Bad Listening Habits   50
How to Help Someone Listen to You   51

PART V   Ten Tips For Tip-Top Listening   55
Take Notes   58
Listen Now, Report Later   58
Learn to Want to Listen   60
Be Present   62
Anticipate Excellence   64
Become a ''Whole-Body'' Listener   66
Build Rapport by Pacing the Speaker   68
Control Your Emotional ''Hot-buttons''   71
Control Distractions   76
Listening is a Gift, Give Generously   78

PART VI   SUMMARY: FIVE POINTS TO REMEMBER   81
Summary   83
Develop A Personal Action Plan   85
Kathy's Story   87

THE BUSINESS OF LISTENING

In Business...

Effective listening lays the foundation for clear understanding

Clear understanding allows an appropriate response

An appropriate response facilitates high quality communication

High quality communication promotes organizational cooperation

Organizational cooperation improves employee morale

High morale increases job commitment

Job commitment leads to peak productivity

Listening is Good Business

P A R T

I

WHY SHOULD YOU LISTEN?

WHAT'S IN IT FOR ME?

At least half of all communication time is spent listening. Experts in a dozen studies have verified that we listen more than any other activity, except breathing. Listening is the "receiving" part of communication. Listening is

- Receiving information through your ears (and eyes).

- Giving meaning to that information.

- Deciding what you think (or feel) about that information.

- Responding to what you hear.

Much of our listening is work related. We spend countless hours of our working lives involved in listening-related activities. Following is a partial list of work-related activities that involve listening. Check those that apply to you.

   ✓   attending meetings, briefings and lectures

   ✓   personal counseling (one-on-one)

   ✓   giving instructions

   ✓   receiving instructions

   ✓   interviewing others

      making decisions based on verbal information

      selling or marketing a product or service

      managing others

      helping clients

      servicing other groups or departments

      using the telephone

WHAT'S IN IT FOR ME? (continued)

If you are like most people, you checked many of the activities on the previous page. What other work-related activities can you think of that involve listening?

_____

_____

_____

_____

_____

What is the business of listening? More important, what's in it for you? Check those items with which you agree:

Listening effectively can

☐ Increase your income.

☐ Improve your company's profits.

☐ Make you more promotable.

☐ Increase your job satisfaction.

☐ Improve your ability to solve problems.

☐ Keep you aware of what is going on in your organization.

BENEFITS OF GOOD LISTENING

THE BENEFITS OF LISTENING—A QUIZ

Read each of the following statements. Write T for true and F for false next to each of the following questions about the benefits of good listening in business relationships. Check your answers with those of the author at the bottom of the page.

1. Skill in listening improves your self confidence.

2. People like you when you listen to them.

3. Good listeners are usually more efficient in completing their work.

4. Careful listening helps to settle disagreements before they escalate.

5. Intelligent responses are easier when you listen.

6. More decisions are made by "shooting from the hip" than by listening to the opinions of others.

7. Learning to listen to clients helps you respond more quickly to their needs.

8. Few good listeners are promoted to top management positions.

9. Good listeners are not often embarrassed by unnecessary mistakes.

10. Handling distractions is difficult for good listeners.

ANSWERS: 1.T 2.T 3.T 4.T 5.T 6.F (Committees, meetings and informal networks are strong evidence that most decisions are made by groups.) 7.T 8.F (Most surveys rank listening as one of the three most important skills of top managers.) 9.T 10.F (Good listeners know how to control distractions by eliminating or ignoring them.)

WHAT'S IN IT FOR ME? (continued)

Successful organizations rely heavily upon listening as an important productivity tool. They seek to hire people who have good listening and communication skills. Employees who know how to listen help their employers by:

- Understanding problems

- Sustaining attention

- Retaining information

- Clarifying procedures

- Building relationships

BUSINESS THRIVES WHEN EMPLOYEES LISTEN

Asleep at the Switch: The Costs of Lazy Listening

Most of us are not good listeners. We listen at about 25 percent of our potential, which means we *ignore, forget, distort* or *misunderstand* 75 percent of what we hear. Hard to believe perhaps, but true. Such lazy listening habits can be very costly, both to our business and to ourselves.

Paul Leat of the Sperry Corporation has stated: ''Poor listening is one of the most significant problems facing business today. Business relies on clear communication. When communication breaks down, costly mistakes are made. Organizations pay for mistakes caused by poor listening with lower profits, and consumers pay for the same mistakes with higher prices.''

Lazy listening is a hidden cost of doing business. Suppose you were employed by a large international company with 10,000 employees. If each person in the company made one $100 error each year, because of poor listening, the company would lose a million dollars. This loss would be especially bad news if your company had a profit sharing plan or was forced to lay off workers due to poor earnings.

The following examples are true stories of the costs of lazy listening.

---

1 A sales manager for a large company asked his accounting department how he could charge off a $100,000 error caused by a dispatcher who routed a fleet of drivers to deliver building material to the wrong state. The dispatcher heard the city (Portland) but not the state (Maine). The result was eight trucks 3,000 miles off course in Portland, Oregon. How could this problem have been avoided?

WHAT'S IN IT FOR ME? (continued)

2 Three computer sales representatives from different companies presented their products to a historian who had special application needs. The historian was a dealer in rare manuscripts and explained to each sales representative what computer functions were required. Two of the sales representatives did not listen and presented products that were inappropriate. The third understood what the historian wanted and she got the order. The manuscript dealer was impressed with only one thing, and it wasn't the hardware because he didn't know much about computers. He did know that two people didn't listen and the third did. He bought his computer from the person who listened. What was the cost to the other two companies?

3 Linda recently cut short a business trip to attend an important investment dinner meeting with her husband. She hurried from the airport, dressed for dinner and met her husband at the restaurant. An hour and a half later their financial advisor had not arrived. A phone call deduced they were at the right restaurant, but on the wrong night. The dinner was rescheduled, but Linda sacrificed profitable business she would have closed had she kept her original trip schedule. How can Linda avoid this problem in the future?

WHAT DO YOU KNOW ABOUT LISTENING?

Write T for true and F for false next to each of the following questions about listening in order to check your present awareness of this important communication skill. See the author's comments at the bottom of the page.

___T___ 1. People who get the facts right are always good listeners.

_____ 2. Listening involves more than your ears.

_____ 3. Hearing is the same as listening.

_____ 4. Good listening comes naturally when we pay attention.

_____ 5. You can listen well and do other things at the same time.

_____ 6. Posture affects listening.

_____ 7. Most listening distractions can be controlled.

_____ 8. If you can't remember something you weren't really listening.

_____ 9. Listening is a passive activity.

_____ 10. Good listeners never interrupt.

Answers: 1. F. (Facts are only part of most messages. Good listeners listen for opinion, emotion and distortion as well.) **2. T.** (To listen well, open your eyes, use your brain, your heart, and your intuition.) **3. F.** (Hearing is the first step, but you must also interpret, evaluate, and respond to the message.) **4. F.** (Paying attention is important, but you must also be able to understand the message, and you must care about the person and/or the message.) **5. F.** (Many people pride themselves in being able to "multi-task," but the more you try to do, the more you scatter your attention. Good listening is focused attention.) **6. T.** (Your body and mind and spirit work together. If your body is slumped and lumpy it gives the mind and spirit the same signals. Remember your parents' and teachers' admonitions: "Sit up and listen!"?) **7. T.** (Most can, but not all. If you are distracted, mention it, move, or do something about it. When that doesn't work, ignore it.) **8. F.** (Yes, memory is an "overlay" of listening, but you may need to remember something for only a short time. We can't consciously remember everything we heard in the past, but if we were able to listen and act on the information effectively at the time, we were listening.) **9. F.** (Listening is anything but passive. You are as responsible as the speaker for successful communication. Your eyes dilate, your palms perspire, and your body is erect. Your mind is active and your energy is focused.) **10. F.** (If the speaker says something you do not understand, interrupt politely and ask for clarification. Otherwise, you will lose the meaning of what follows. Taking notes helps.)

WHY SHOULD WE LISTEN?

Why should we listen? What are the advantages of overcoming lazy listening habits and changing unproductive ways of listening? List as many reasons as you can think of in the space below. Place a ☑ next to those that are most important to you. Then read ''Fifty Good Reasons to Become a Better Listener'' on the facing page. Check any you would like to add to your list.

REASONS FOR ME TO BECOME A BETTER LISTENER

FIFTY GOOD REASONS TO BECOME A BETTER LISTENER

1. To learn something.
2. To be entertained.
3. To understand a situation.
4. To get information.
5. To be courteous.
6. To be responsible.
7. To prevent accidents.
8. To be a team player.
9. To ask intelligent questions.
10. To improve confidence.
11. To protect freedom.
12. To find out people's needs.
13. To negotiate effectively.
14. To be valued and trusted.
15. To use money wisely.
16. To be more efficient and productive.
17. To evaluate accurately.
18. To make comparisons.
19. To share in your children's lives.
20. To analyze the speaker's purpose.
21. To be liked by others.
22. To get the best value.
23. To improve self-discipline.
24. To build relationships.

FIFTY GOOD REASONS TO BECOME
A BETTER LISTENER (continued)

25. To solve problems.

26. To show compassion.

27. To satisfy curiosity.

28. To be safe.

29. To be a good lover.

30. To make intelligent decisions.

31. To prevent waste.

32. To make money.

33. To avoid embarrassment.

34. To stay out of trouble.

35. To save time.

36. To be an informed consumer.

37. To be a supportive friend.

38. To give an appropriate response.

39. To enjoy the sounds of nature.

40. To create ''win-win'' situations.

41. To control distractions.

42. To increase concentration.

43. To improve your vocabulary.

44. To stay healthy.

45. To be prepared for sudden shifts in a speaker's topic or intention.

46. To be a better family member.

47. To settle disagreements.

48. To maintain a flexible attitude.

49. To improve your personality.

50. To use the gift of hearing.

THE JOY OF SMALL CHANGE

To improve the listening skills suggested in this book, we must be both motivated and educated. We must believe that each small change in lazy listening habits has value for us.

Change can be hard work. Setbacks sometimes occur just when we think we're making progress. To change our listening habits we must believe that the new skills we are gaining are worth more to us than the unproductive habits we are giving up. As you work to change your behavior and practice the listening techniques presented in the pages ahead, the following suggestions will be helpful. To effectively change, it is recommended that you:

1. **Notice small changes.** Recognize your improvements and give yourself a pat on the back as they occur. Acknowledging improvements is a form of positive reinforcement.

2. **Keep a log of significant listening habit changes**—such as:

   • Paying attention in a dull meeting.

   • Receiving positive feedback from your manager about your communication skills.

   • Preventing yourself from interrupting a co-worker at coffee.

3. **Acknowledge setbacks but do not give in to them.** Failure to learn from mistakes is the only real failure.

4. **Stay with it.** Unless you consciously work to improve your listening skills, you will find it easy to slip back into your old, bad habits.

P A R T

II

FOUR KEY ELEMENTS OF GOOD LISTENING

HOW TO BE A GOOD LISTENER

Good listening is an active integrated communication skill that demands energy and know-how. It is purposeful, powerful and productive. To listen effectively we must *hear* and *select* information from the speaker, *give it meaning, determine how we feel about it* and *respond*—in a matter of seconds!

We must also understand the speaker's purpose to know how to listen most effectively. The speaker's purpose influences the way we listen and how we perceive what is said. The speaker and the listener must have the same purpose if communication is to be effective. Next time you are listening to someone, make sure you are aware of the speaker's purpose. Is he or she:

    ____ Entertaining you?

    ____ Providing critical data?

    ____ Persuading you?

    ____ Sharing feelings?

    ____ Making small talk?

For example, if Joe is making small talk, you can enjoy the conversation for its own sake. You and Joe are building rapport and strengthening your relationship with this casual conversation. However, if you are in a meeting with Joe, and he is informing you of important changes in inventory procedure, you will be listening for facts, contrasts, numbers and other key information. You will probably be taking notes and you will ask questions to clarify what you do not understand.

On the following pages are the four key elements of the listening process. They describe what good listeners do to listen more effectively in any situation. After each element is a "Listening Lab" that contains suggestions and exercises to improve your listening skills.

ARE YOU A GOOD LISTENER?

Before reading the elements of good listening, consider what you already know about yourself as a listener. Remember that we listen differently at different times to different people. Evaluate yourself at the beginning of this section, then put a date on your calendar two weeks from today and evaluate again, to see if any of your numbers change. They will change positively if you commit to doing something about negative listening habits. It's up to you.

Following are ten characteristics of a good listener. On a scale of 1–5, with five being the highest, fill in the blank to indicate the degree to which you already practice these positive listening behaviors. Go through the list twice, first rating yourself with the person you listen to the best, then rating yourself with the person to whom you find it most difficult to listen.

	BEST	WORST	
1.	_____	_____	I make regular eye contact with the speaker.
2.	_____	_____	I ask questions for clarification.
3.	_____	_____	I show concern by acknowledging feelings.
4.	_____	_____	I restate or paraphrase some of the speaker's words to show that I understand.
5.	_____	_____	I seek first to understand, then to be understood.
6.	_____	_____	I am poised and emotionally controlled.
7.	_____	_____	I react nonverbally, with a smile, a nod, a frown, or a touch, if appropriate.
8.	_____	_____	I pay close attention and do not let my mind wander.
9.	_____	_____	I act responsibly on what I hear.
10.	_____	_____	I don't change the subject without warning.

Following is a list of ten bad habits of listening. On a scale of 1–5, with five being the worst case, indicate the degree to which you are guilty of these poor listening habits. Rate yourself twice, first with the person you listen to the best, then with the person to whom you find it most difficult to listen. Be honest with yourself. Recognizing *how* you listen is the first step toward constructive change.

BEST   **WORST**

1. _____ _____ I interrupt often.

2. _____ _____ I jump to conclusions.

3. _____ _____ I finish other people's sentences.

4. _____ _____ I am parental, and answer with advice.

5. _____ _____ I make up my mind before I have all of the information.

6. _____ _____ I am a compulsive note taker.

7. _____ _____ I don't give any response.

8. _____ _____ I am impatient.

9. _____ _____ I lose my temper.

10. _____ _____ I think about my reply while the other person is speaking.

FOUR KEY ELEMENTS OF GOOD LISTENING
KEY ELEMENT #1

HEAR THE MESSAGE

Our brain recognizes sound as it enters the ear. Then, other "listening channels" such as our eyes and our feelings seek confirmation of the message from the speaker's nonverbal feedback, such as body language and tone of voice. Hearing is the *beginning* of the listening process. It is nonselective and involuntary. However, when you *choose* to listen, it is on purpose.

LISTENING IS VOLUNTARY

From the constant noise around us, we select what we want to listen to. This information moves from Short Term Memory (STM) to Long Term Memory (LTM). Short Term Memory is a "holding pen" for incoming signals from our five senses. In order to protect us from too much stimulation STM has a limited capacity and is easily disrupted. For instance, a mail clerk would not likely retain much information from a technical discussion about Data Transport Protocols because he/she would have no use for the message. The information would probably be held in STM for 1-30 seconds and then dismissed. If the information we hear is not recognized and selected for processing, it is dismissed from STM and not remembered.

In a sense, we are preprogrammed. Our choices of what to listen to come from previous choices based on interests and needs. John enjoys investing in stocks and bonds, so he always has his "ears open" for tips on the market. Ellie "tunes in" whenever someone is discussing consumer rights. Ralph "catches" the football scores each Saturday to track his favorite teams. In other words, we choose what we want to listen to and often it is based on our past choices.

In order to listen to a speaker, we begin by *hearing* and *selecting* oral messages, and accompanying nonverbal signals. When these messages are interesting or important, we pay attention to them.

We choose to listen because

- The message is important

- We are interested

- We feel like listening

- We listened to this kind of information in the past

- We like/respect the person speaking

Sometimes, even when we choose to listen, anger, frustration, grief or hostility can act as "emotional cotton" in our ears. We tend to hear what we expect, or want to hear, and filter out that which is not consistent with our feelings and attitudes. For example, Jennifer was on her way to lunch when her manager dropped a report on her desk and said he needed twenty sets of copies when he returned from lunch. Jennifer was upset because her friends were waiting and she assumed she had to make the copies. She did not hear her boss say after *his* lunch, which was an hour later than hers. If she had listened carefully, she would have had ample time to make the copies after she returned from her lunch.

THREE KEYS TO HEARING THE MESSAGE

CARE

PAY ATTENTION

SELECT WHAT IS IMPORTANT

22

LISTENING LAB: KEY ELEMENT #1
—HEAR THE MESSAGE

Exercise 1.

Sit quietly someplace where people are talking around you: hotel lobby, office corridor, restaurant, airport. Listen for about ten minutes and then write down what you heard, (i.e., what people said, and other incidental sounds or noises). This activity should make you conscious of the many voices and sounds that bombard you daily. It reminds you that listening begins with hearing, but it is a voluntary activity.

1. What did you hear?

2. How many sounds do you remember?

3. What sounds did you remember most easily?

4. Did your mind wander while you were listening?

5. Try the experiment again with your eyes closed and see if the results are the same. (You will notice how important your eyes are to listening.)

AUTHORS COMMENTS

1. We hear sounds constantly, but remember few.

2. We remember sounds that are important, interesting or unusual.

3. Same as #2.

4. We all daydream frequently. We cannot remember what we did not hear.

5. People sometimes complain they cannot listen as well when they are not wearing glasses because they cannot see the speaker's nonverbal message.

EXERCISE 2.

Listed below are some methods for improving listening at the "hearing" level. Write any others you can think of. Select one specific method to work on for the next three days. At the end of the three days, assign yourself a grade (A, B, C, D, E) for how well you did.

- Improving your listening vocabulary so that words and meanings are clear when you listen.

- Having your hearing checked.

- Asking for repetition or clarification.

- Overcoming a tendency to daydream.

- Eliminating distractions.

Others:

- _____

- _____

- _____

- _____

- _____

KEY ELEMENT #2

INTERPRET THE MESSAGE

Interpreting a speaker's message means coming to a mutual understanding of the speaker's meaning. Good listeners know that a match-up in meaning is a match-up in understanding. The word communication comes from the Latin root word **communis** which means "commonness," a commonness of understanding.

Listeners often experience problems at the interpreting level because no two people perceive a message in the same way. Speakers do not always say exactly what they mean, or mean exactly what they say.

> **WHAT IS THE DIFFERENCE?**
> "When I look at you, time stands still."
> "You have a face that would stop a clock."

We probably do not interpret accurately in most listening situations. Listening is a complicated process. Speakers send messages to listeners both verbally and nonverbally. If Jim tells Rod, "You have to do something about the Doughty account," Rod must assign meaning to Jim's **words, filters, tone of voice** and **nonverbal cues.**

WORDS   Words themselves have little meaning. They are merely vehicles for the thoughts and feelings of the speaker. Words are not actual experiences, but a means of explaining experiences. It is people who give meaning to words.

FILTERS   Both listeners and speakers have filters, which help or hinder the interpreting process. These filters are in our brains ''data base,'' and they attach personal meaning to information as it is presented. Some examples of filters include the following; *can you add others?*

memories	current attention span	language and vocabulary
perceptions	past experiences	needs and motives
biases	values	age
attitudes	knowledge and intelligence	sensory acuity
expectations	feelings	assumptions
emotional hot-buttons		

TONE OF VOICE   Voice conveys approximately 30 percent of the meaning of a message. Voices can be insistent, pleading, questioning, whining, demanding, etc. Tom speaks in a quiet monotone. Even though he is intelligent, his voice lacks conviction, and people don't take him seriously. What could Tom do with his voice to get people to listen to him?

NONVERBAL CUES   A nonverbal cue, or body language, is a message sent by such things as a speaker's gestures, facial expressions, eyes and posture. Good listeners interpret a speaker's nonverbal feedback through five channels: *ears, eyes, heart, mind* and *intuition*. Nonverbal cues, along with tone of voice, confirm or deny the message of the words. More than half of most human interaction is through nonverbal communication.

Good listeners who aren't sure of the speaker's meaning will ask for repetition or clarification (feedback).

''Is this what you mean when you say...?''

''This is how I interpret what you are saying...Am I correct?''

''I'm not sure I understand your meaning, could you be more specific?''

```
THREE KEYS TO INTERPRETING THE MESSAGE
       UNDERSTANDING YOUR FILTERS
       USING ALL FIVE CHANNELS
       ASKING FOR CLARIFICATION
```

LISTENING LAB: KEY ELEMENT #2
—INTERPRET THE MESSAGE

EXERCISE 1.

Let us imagine you have just interviewed a young woman for an important sales position in your department. As she is leaving she remembers one last thing she wants you to know, and states: ''By the way, I graduated in the top 10 percent of my class.'' She then shakes your hand, thanks you for the interview and leaves. Following are some interpretations of her statement. Read these, then list several other possible interpretations of her statement.

> ''By the way, I graduated in the top 10 percent of my class.''

1. She is intelligent.

2. She is competitive.

3. The school was not academically challenging.

4. She studied constantly.

5. She was bragging.

6. _____

7. _____

How would you clarify your interpretation?*

EXERCISE 2.

Say the following sentence out loud seven times. I NEVER SAID YOU STOLE THE MONEY. Each time you say it, emphasize a different word. For example, the first time through, emphasize the word *I. I* never said you stole the money. This example shows how voice emphasis influences our interpretation of information. To become a better communicator, listen carefully to the speaker's voice inflection and word emphasis.

---

*Comments: Good listeners want to understand the speaker's meaning. They are aware of their own filters and those of the speaker, and they ask *questions when they need clarification.*

KEY ELEMENT #3

EVALUATE THE MESSAGE

Good listeners make sure they have all of the key information before forming an opinion. They do not jump to conclusions based on a bias or incomplete information. They may agree or disagree with the speaker. Good listening does not mean automatic compliance. A good listener will weigh and analyze all of the evidence before reaching a final decision or making a written or verbal judgment.

> Diana is a member of a jury trying a felony case. As each attorney sifts through the evidence, Diana listens carefully for validation of her opinions. She is careful not to jump to conclusions based on emotional testimony. At the conclusion of the trial Diana evaluates all of the evidence presented by both sides before making a statement about her decision. The jury foreman later thanked Diana for her valuable observations and objective comments.

We make conscientious evaluations when we make decisions based on *all* of the available information. We run into problems with evaluation when we think mechanically, or jump to conclusions. We must ask ourselves if we are listening *to* someone or listening *against* them. Are we *evaluating* or making a *value judgment*?

Evaluation is not required in every listening situation, therefore, we must also know our purpose for listening.

THREE KEYS TO EVALUATING THE MESSAGE

ASK QUESTIONS

ANALYZE THE EVIDENCE

DON'T JUMP TO CONCLUSIONS

LISTENING LAB: KEY ELEMENT #3
—EVALUATE THE MESSAGE

You listen constantly to advertising on radio and television. How often do you stop to evaluate the slant or bias of advertisers who want to buy their services or products? How often do you ask if the information is reasonable and logical? Do you ask yourself what they are *not* telling you? Following is a description of Adolph Hitler, as it may have been written by his press agent. Read the description, as if you were listening to it, taking note of the press agent's built-in bias. Then answer the questions that follow.

"Our leader had an unhappy childhood and little formal education. His father bitterly opposed his ambition to become an artist. Through self-education, he became the author of a book, that became a national bestseller. Obstacles did not discourage him. When others say, "That is not possible," he hurdles each barrier as it comes. He has built an active youth movement of selected young people. He is known throughout the world for his dynamic speeches. His closest associates say of him, "He accomplishes great deeds out of the passion of his will in order to create the kind of government he believes in.""

1. How would you evaluate Hitler if you had not heard of him before you read this description?

2. Are any character flaws suggested in the description?

3. What methods does the press agent use to create a positive impression of Hitler?

4. How can this exercise help you evaluate information more carefully?

KEY ELEMENT #4

RESPOND TO THE MESSAGE

Although a response may be considered a speaking rather than a listening role, it is critical to clear communication. The listener must let the speaker know by verbal and/or nonverbal feedback what was heard and how it was heard. Good listeners accept responsibility to provide feedback to the speaker to complete the communication process.

Good listeners have a strong desire to reach a common understanding. Confident responses inform the speaker that:

1. The message was heard.
2. It was understood.
3. It was evaluated appropriately.

Several problems can occur in this key element. One is when no response occurs. If Karla asks Jack when the plans for the new office building will be available, and Jack simply looks at Karla without indicating that he heard her, he is not communicating effectively. Although silence can communicate, a blank stare is not a confident response. Other problems include responses that are defensive, overly emotional or inappropriate. If Jack had abruptly changed the subject, his response would have been inappropriate also. Finally, a confusing response (i.e. a double message) can occur when the verbal and nonverbal are in conflict.

If Jack had smiled in a friendly manner, but his voice sounded hostile as he replied, ''Why do *you* want to know?'' he would have confused Karla. He was sending her two messages: one with his voice and one with his smile. Double messages are difficult to decode. They are often sent by someone who is afraid of the consequences of telling the truth.

THREE KEYS TO RESPONDING TO THE MESSAGE

WANT TO REACH A COMMON UNDERSTANDING

GIVE FEEDBACK VERBALLY AND/OR NONVERBALLY

AVOID CONFUSING MESSAGES

LISTENING LAB: KEY ELEMENT #4
—RESPOND TO THE MESSAGE.

Following are several possible responses in listening situations. Place a check next to those you think are important for good communication.

☐ Providing prompt feedback.

☐ Giving feedback that is relevant to the conversation.

☐ Changing the subject.

☐ Interrupting by waving your arms or stamping your feet.

☐ Using appropriate eye contact.

☐ Combining verbal and nonverbal (body language) feedback for more complete communication.

☐ Staring blankly.

☐ Asking a question for clarification.

☐ Mumbling.

Add you own responsible responses below:

REVIEW LAB FOR KEY ELEMENTS 1–4

Review each of the key elements in the listening process. Then make a date for coffee with a co-worker and carefully notice yourself going through the four steps when it is your turn to listen.

After your coffee date, the following checklist will help you focus on each key element and evaluate your awareness of your listening behavior. Check each answer that applies to you.

Review Lab for Key Element #1 — Hearing the Message

During our conversation, did I . . .

☐ care about my co-worker's attitudes, opinions and beliefs?

☐ pay close attention?

☐ ask for clarification when I didn't understand something?

☐ allow myself to become distracted?

☐ seek to understand the feelings behind the words?

☐ listen carefully enough to remember what my co-worker said?

Three specific points made by my co-worker.

_____

_____

_____

Review Lab for Key Element #2 — Interpreting the Message

During our conversation, did I . . .

☐ notice any words that were used in an unusual context?

☐ ask questions for clarification?

☐ pay attention to his or her tone of voice?

☐ watch for nonverbal cues such as facial expression or gestures?

☐ notice if the body language, tone and words all conveyed the same message?

☐ let my own filters interfere with my co-worker's meaning?

Two questions I asked in order to make sure that I understood my co-worker's meaning:

_____

_____

REVIEW LAB FOR KEY ELEMENTS 1–4 (Continued)

Review Lab for Key Element #3 — Evaluating the Message

During our conversation, did I . . .

☐ believe everything I heard?

☐ agree with everything I heard?

☐ disagree agreeably?

☐ weigh and analyze all of the information before responding?

☐ jump to conclusions?

☐ ask questions when I needed more information?

☐ evaluate the information rather than judge the person?

I evaluated two of my co-worker's statements as follows:

_____

_____

_____

_____

Review Lab for Key Element #4 — Responding to the Message

During our conversation, did I . . .

☐ take responsibility for my responses?

☐ look and act interested?

☐ repeat information for clarity?

☐ rush the speaker?

I took responsibility for my responses in the following ways:

_____

_____

_____

_____

P A R T

III

YOUR LISTENING STYLE: A BARRIER OR A BRIDGE

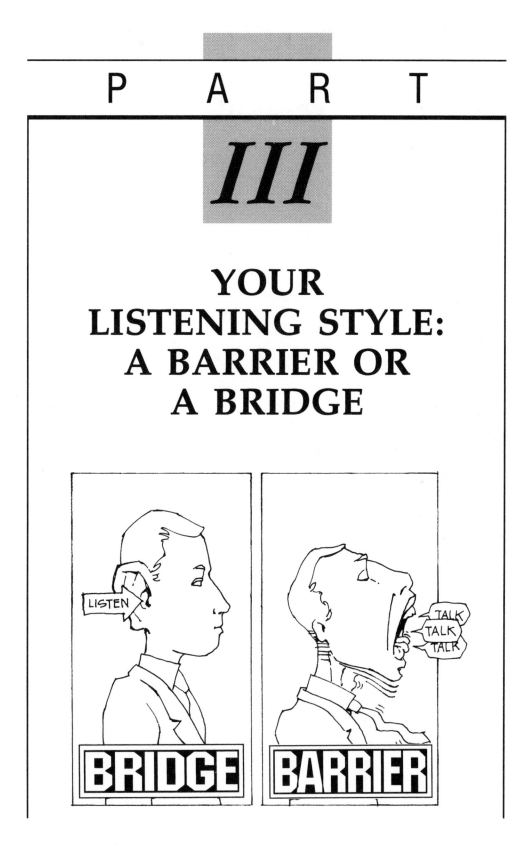

BARRIERS TO COMMUNICATION

Listening style reflects the attitude and behavior of the listener. It is *how* an individual listens. Your listening style can be a *bridge* or a *barrier* to good communication. Listeners can avoid the barriers of listening by being aware of what the pitfalls are and knowing how to avoid them.

Following are some descriptions of listening styles. Answer the questions following each description in order to help these "characters" improve their listening styles.

VACANT VINCENT

The most difficult person to communicate with is a daydreamer. Meet Vacant Vincent. You will recognize him by the faraway look in his eyes. Vincent is like a social butterfly who dips in and out of conversations picking up bits and pieces of information. He is physically present but not really there. Vincent is easily distracted and often changes the subject without warning. Sometimes he slouches, as if he is tired. He plays with his tie or impatiently taps his pencil on the desk. The best way to get Vincent's attention is to talk about *his* interests.

How can Vincent become a better listener? Following is a list of possible behaviors. Check any that would help Vincent improve his communication skills.

1. ____ Sitting in a listening position
2. ____ Making eye contact
3. ____ Controlling distractions
4. ____ Playing with his computer
5. ____ Fidgeting
6. ____ Sticking to the subject
7. ____ Taking an interest in other people
8. ____ Losing his temper

BARRIERS TO COMMUNICATION (continued)

CRITICAL CARRIE

Critical listening is important in management, especially when problems need to be solved, but some managers listen only to find fault. Critical Carrie listens for the facts, but is so critical of each item that she often misses "the big picture." She seldom spends time with her staff, but when she does she is usually issuing orders. She asks abrupt questions and cuts off people before they can respond fully as she listens to elements of a problem. Her questions are demanding and make her co-workers feel cornered. Carrie frowns or rolls her eyes in disbelief and is quick to place blame. Critical Carrie is an incessant note taker, so her eye contact is limited. She finds little time for small talk. Her staff wishes she would "lighten up" and not jump to conclusions so quickly. Because she seldom listens to them, her staff avoids her. They long ago stopped sharing information with her because "she doesn't listen anyway."

What would help Carrie communicate more effectively with her staff? Following is a list of possible behaviors. Check any that would help Carrie improve her listening style.

1. ____ Building rapport with "small talk"
2. ____ Listening for the "big picture"
3. ____ Taking more notes
4. ____ Showing interest in her employees

5. ____ Creating an atmosphere of mistrust
6. ____ Learning karate
7. ____ Developing patience
8. ____ Learning to smile.

Answers: 1, 2, 4, 6, 7.

COMPLIANT CURTIS

Compliant listening is a passive behavior that does not allow the speaker to understand the real feelings or opinions of the listener. Listeners such as Compliant Curtis listen much more than they talk. In many cases, they are shy. They want to please others and keep communications pleasant. Compulsive talkers often seek out listeners like Compliant Curtis, because they need people with the patience to listen to them. Unfortunately, when Curtis speaks, he usually keeps his *real* opinions to himself for fear of criticism. Sometimes he fakes attention as he silently thinks his private thoughts. In meetings Curtis nods his head approvingly, but adds little to the discussion. You will recognize Compliant Curtis by such phrases as ''That's nice,'' or ''I see your point.''

How can Curtis become a more involved listener? Check any of the following behaviors that would help him improve his listening style.

1. ____ Voicing his opinions
2. ____ Working to develop positive assertiveness*
3. ____ Daydreaming
4. ____ Asking questions
5. ____ Listening more intently
6. ____ Mentally finishing other people's sentences
7. ____ Speaking with conviction
8. ____ Avoiding eye contact

*For an excellent self-study book on this topic order *Developing Positive Assertiveness* from the back of this book.

Answers: 1, 2, 4, 5, 7.

BRIDGES TO COMMUNICATION

"Active" listening is the bridge to good communication. It is committed listening based on good habits and self control. Good listening is purposeful and productive because it allows the listener and the speaker to reach understanding. Following are descriptions of active listening styles that create positive communication.

ARLO ACTIVE

Arlo Active, a skilled training director, is an involved listener. He is "present" and participative and assumes responsibility for the success of communications in his department. In meetings and discussions Arlo requires discipline and relevance from his employees and bridges gaps in understanding by asking questions for clarification. Individuals in his department appreciate Arlo's clear verbal *and* nonverbal responses and focused eye contact. Arlo tries to see the other person's point of view, and he refrains from evaluating information too quickly. As an active listener, Arlo listens not only to the *content* of employees' statements, but also to their *intent*.

LISETTE LISTENER

Lisette Listener, a successful real estate agent, credits her success to purposeful listening. When interviewing potential clients, Lisette listens carefully to their requirements for a home. She pays close attention to where they want to live, the desired style of house and the value they place on schools and services. She asks many questions for clarification. She then "feeds back" what she hears to be sure she is accurate in her interpretation. By the end of a busy "listening" day Lisette often feels as tired as if she had built a house, rather than sold one. She realizes that active listening is hard work, but she knows her results are measured clearly by her commissions, her satisfied new home owners and the new friends she makes.

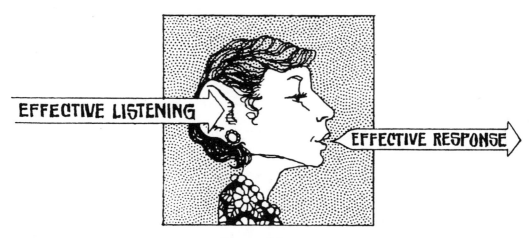

Lisette Listener

BARRIERS AND BRIDGES TO COMMUNICATION (continued)

What other listening styles (positive and negative) can you think of?

Listening Styles	Style	Attitude Conveyed	Verbal or Nonverbal Behavior
Positive			
Negative			

P A R T

IV

HOW WELL
DO YOU
LISTEN?

A LISTENING ATTITUDE: YOUR KEY TO SUCCESS

What kind of a listener are you? Conscientious? Rushed? Thoughtful? Interruptive? This section provides you with some self-evaluation tools. What is your listening attitude? How well does it contribute to your overall success in business? In your personal life?

Most people believe they are effective listeners. However, as previously noted, research indicates that on average we are effective listeners at only a 25 percent efficiency level. Much of the time we *think* we are listening. We seem to believe because we have ears we are listening. This is like believing that because we have eyes we can read. Undiagnosed bad habits such as interrupting, allowing ourselves to be distracted, jumping to conclusions, daydreaming or giving in to boredom prevent us from becoming the kind of listeners we think we are. The only way for us to progress is to make some conscious changes.

Change begins with an honest self-evaluation of our strengths *and* weaknesses. The exercises in this section will allow you to evaluate your listening style and plan a strategy for change.

Practicing the exercises in this section will make you a better listener. First, identify your listening problems and decide which changes you want to make. To be effective, plan positive action steps, and then practice specific listening skills at every opportunity. This will dramatically improve your ability to listen more effectively. Turn the page so you can begin to identify, plan and practice skills to improve your listening.

A LISTENING ATTITUDE:
YOUR KEY TO SUCCESS (continued)

Developing listening skills is an ongoing process. Discovering your attitude about listening is an important first step toward personal success. Attitudes determine our behaviors. To discover your listening attitudes, complete the following exercise. If a statement describes your listening attitude or behavior check "Yes," if not, check "No." Be honest.

LISTENING ATTITUDES AND BEHAVIORS

	YES	NO
1. I am interested in many subjects and do not knowingly tune out dry-sounding information.	☐	☐
2. I listen carefully for a speaker's main ideas and supporting points.	☐	☐
3. I take notes during meetings to record key points.	☐	☐
4. I am not easily distracted.	☐	☐
5. I keep my emotions under control.	☐	☐
6. I do not fake attention.	☐	☐
7. I wait for the speaker to finish before finally evaluating the message.	☐	☐
8. I respond appropriately with a smile, a nod or a word of acknowledgment as a speaker is talking.	☐	☐
9. I am aware of mannerisms that may distract a speaker and keep mine under control.	☐	☐
10. I understand my biases and control them when I am listening.	☐	☐

	YES	NO
11. I refrain from constantly interrupting.	☐	☐
12. I value eye contact and maintain it most of the time.	☐	☐
13. I often restate or paraphrase what the speaker said to make sure I have the correct meaning.	☐	☐
14. I listen for the speaker's emotional meaning as well as subject matter content.	☐	☐
15. I ask questions for clarification.	☐	☐
16. I do not finish other people's sentences unless asked to do so.	☐	☐
17. When listening on the telephone, I keep one hand free to take notes.	☐	☐
18. I attempt to set aside my ego and focus on the speaker rather than on myself.	☐	☐
19. I am careful to judge the message rather than the speaker.	☐	☐
20. I am a patient listener most of the time.	☐	☐

The following scale will help you interpret your present listening skill level based on your current attitudes and behaviors.

1-5 "No" answers	You are an excellent listener. Keep it up!
6-10 "No" answers	You are a good listener, but can improve.
11-15 "No" answers	Through practice you can become a much more effective listener in your business and personal relationships.
16-20 "No" answers	Listen up!

46

PERSONAL LISTENING INVENTORY

The Personal Listening Inventory on the facing page will help you rate yourself as a listener. An interpretation of results follows this inventory. When you have completed it you will have a better insight into:

How much time you spend listening.

How you rate yourself as a listener.

How you think others rate you as a listener.

How you rate others as listeners.

PERSONAL LISTENING INVENTORY

1. On a scale of 1-10 (with 10 being highest), how committed are you to improving your listening? _____

2. On average, what percentage of each business day do you spend listening? _____

3. On a scale of 1-10 (with 10 being highest), how would you rate yourself as a listener? _____

4. On a scale of 1-10, how would you rate the best listener you know? _____

5. On a scale of 1-10, how would you rate the worst listener you know? _____

6. On a scale of 1-10 (with 10 being highest), how would the following people (where appropriate) rate you as a listener?

    Manager _____   Spouse/Lover _____

    Subordinate _____   Child(ren) _____

    Close colleague _____   Best friend _____

For the author's interpretation of the Personal Listening Inventory see the next page.

PERSONAL LISTENING INVENTORY— AUTHOR RESPONSES

The following interpretation of the Personal Listening Inventory you took on page 47 will help you compare your results with those of others.

1. We need to become committed to becoming better listeners, because **listening is hard work.** It requires patience, persistence and a plan for improvement. Casual involvement and genuine commitment are not the same thing. Suppose you had ham and eggs for breakfast. The chicken was involved in the meal, but the pig was committed. What is your commitment to your listening improvement?

2. According to experts we spend approximately 80 percent of each business day communicating. Of that time, 45 percent is spent listening, 30 percent speaking, 16 percent reading and 9 percent writing. A manager may spend up to 60 percent of each business day listening.

3. Most people listen at about 50 percent efficiency during the first part of an oral communication. In other words, if tested immediately on what they just heard, they would accurately remember 50 percent. However, the efficiency rate drops quickly after the initial statements. Most people average a 25 percent efficiency rate overall.

4. Best listeners are usually rated as 8, 9 or 10. This is higher than most individuals rate themselves. The best listeners are often mentors, role models or professional counselors.

5. Worst listeners are usually rated at 0–4. This score is much lower than most people rate themselves. ''Worst listeners'' are often related to us, probably because we save our worst behaviors for the people closest to us.

6. It is not unusual to discover that our best friends rate us highest and our family lowest. Subordinates and colleagues rank us about the same as we rank ourselves. Bosses usually rank us higher than we rank ourselves because we listen better to them than to others. In other words, we are more attentive when there is a direct payoff or penalty.

YOUR LISTENING QUALITIES: AN AWARENESS EXERCISE

1. List five of your best listening qualities, such as patience, good eye contact, not jumping to conclusions, asking for clarification, etc. Rank them 1-5, with one (1) being your best quality.

    1.

    2.

    3.

    4.

    5.

2. List three listening qualities that you don't have now but would like to have.

    1.

    2.

    3.

3. List five of your worst listening qualities, such as impatience, poor eye contact, jumping to conclusions, not asking for clarification, etc. Rank them, with one (1) being the worst, etc.

    1.

    2.

    3.

    4.

    5.

4. List three listening qualities, of poor listeners you know, that you would like to avoid. Make a commitment to be more patient with those people, and not fall into those behaviors yourself.

    1.

    2.

    3.

Now turn to the next page to see how to eliminate bad listening habits and replace them with good ones.

HOW TO STOMP BAD LISTENING HABITS

1. **Catch yourself in the act.** Recognition is the first step for preventive maintenance. By listing the listening habits you want to eliminate on the previous page, you should be able to more readily recognize them. By monitoring your listening behavior you can catch yourself when you fall into an undesirable behavior, then take steps toward positive change. Remember, you must *want* to change or you will not make the effort.

2. **Fight the habit.** Don't tolerate what you want to eliminate from your listening style. Stomp it. Drop it. Change your ways! Like a smoker kicking the habit, cold turkey is the best way. Don't wait until next time to do things differently. Admit your behavior (i.e., ''I just interrupted you. I'm sorry, please go on with what you were saying.'') This is a way of catching yourself in the act and acknowledging your bad habit.

3. **Substitute the old habit with a new habit.** Memorize the list of new habits you want to develop. If you are chronically impatient, find a way to learn patience. For example, think about how you appreciate other people's patience when you are trying to explain something, then act the way you were treated. Visualize yourself as being patient, or not interrupting, or listening without daydreaming, etc. Look for the value in the new behavior you select and trust yourself to do it.

4. **Acknowledge your success.** When you successfully substitute an improved listening behavior, give yourself a reward—a pat on the back. Put five dollars toward a vacation fund, or a star in your listening diary. Say to yourself ''I did it!'' Tell someone to see if they praise you; or better yet, tell someone you know *will* praise you.

5. **Be patient with yourself.** Why is it that we are more tolerant of other people's mistakes than of our own? Cut yourself some slack. In other words, give yourself a break and be realistic when you set your listening goals. Self-improvement is a life-long project, and the road to success is always under construction. There's no such thing as perfect listening; but we can all improve.

HOW TO HELP SOMEONE LISTEN TO YOU

Much of this book is focused on how *you* can become a better listener. And although your skills may improve, how do you help others improve their skills? How do you get them to listen to you?

The hard truth is that we can only be responsible for our own listening. If we listen respectfully and model good listening behavior we are more likely to be listened to. However, some people are not attentive listeners, despite your good example. In this case, be assertive and ask them to listen. Ask politely and with good will. If you don't mention the problem, chances are they will continue to listen haphazardly, because lousy listeners don't usually know they are doing anything wrong. They are both unskilled and uninformed.

Statements to help people listen:

"I feel that I'm not being listened to (heard)."

"This information is important and I need to know that you are hearing me. So I need your undivided attention."

"Please listen to me."

"I feel (ignored, angry, unimportant to you) when you don't listen."

"Let me repeat what I just said, as it is important that you hear me."

Following are suggestions that will make it easier for others to *want* to listen to you. Check those with which you agree.

☐ **I am interested in the thoughts and opinions of others.**

People don't care what you know until they know you care. Do you listen to others in the way that you like to be listened to? Don't expect others to listen to you if you are heedless or overly critical of their ideas and attitudes. Respect must be mutual for good communication to thrive.

HOW TO HELP SOMEONE LISTEN TO YOU (continued)

☐ I am interesting to talk to.

I have a few hobbies, go to the movies, read the paper or like sports. I know what is happening on television and in the world. I have traveled. I tell good stories and I know a few jokes appropriate for mixed audiences. I speak clearly and distinctly, and I use good English. I don't repeat myself. I do not sprinkle my vocabulary with colorful epithets (swearing). I have one or two areas of expertise about which I can speak with some authority (carpentry, computers, raising dogs, etc.). I am enthusiastic. I don't speak in a monotone or sound bored. If I am shy, I try to believe in myself and to express my opinions more often. (If you feel that others wouldn't be interested in hearing what you have to say because you are a little boring, take a Dale Carnegie course. It can't hurt.)

☐ I tell the truth.

Remember the old adage: "If you tell the truth, you won't have to remember what you said." Everyone has a good "baloney barometer" and exaggeration and white lies are seldom tolerated for long.

☐ I avoid "bigshotitis" and namedropping.

Familiar references to famous people or high-ranking officials are appropriate if we know them well, otherwise we are using their names to make ourselves look important. Putting ourselves in a "one-up" position means that the listener is in a "one-down" position. Then communication becomes competition.

☐ I am my authentic self.

You are the first best you, and the second best anyone else. Being comfortable with being you is the greatest gift you can give yourself. You are unique. Let that be enough. Pretense is a result of trying to be like someone else because we don't like who we are. When we are settled with ourselves, others find us more approachable and likeable.

☐ I am conscious of timing and preliminary tuning.

I prepare my listener for what I am going to say. For example: "You should know the counts for both kinds of cholesterol when you have your cholesterol level tested. Let me say why I think that." Be aware of the processing time needed by your listener. Be patient. Some people are internal processors and take extra time to think before they respond. External processors respond rapidly, but they may not respond as clearly or accurately.

☐ **I get to the point.**

Keep the message moving. Too much detail kills interest. Keep your listener stimulated by providing new ideas, adding colorful words, anecdotes and visual images. Avoid jargon, cliches and hackneyed phrases. Be specific and be clear. Don't force assumptions. Fill in the background, but avoid endless detail. When possible, plan what you will say to make it easy for your listener.

☐ **I am sensitive to my listener's needs.**

Don't drop verbal bombs when the listener is in the wrong physical or psychological state. Break bad news gently. It isn't what you say, it is how you say it. Outline your message. "Our financial picture is somewhat bleak for next quarter. Here are three ideas for coping with the problem." Say the vital parts first and last. People seldom remember what is in the middle.

☑ **I use my listener's name regularly.**

People love to hear their own names. Use them often in your communication and give others credit for their ideas and suggestions. Ask them questions and seek feedback about their opinions.

☐ **I use good eye communication.**

Really seeing people is very different from just looking at them. Use verbal and nonverbal signals to let your listeners know that you want to talk *with* them, rather than *at* them.

Take the time to honestly evaluate your communication skills. Our personal attitudes, habits and intentions greatly affect the way others listen to us.

P A R T

V

TEN TIPS FOR TIP-TOP LISTENING

10 TIPS

1.
2.
3.
4.
5.
6.
7.
8.
9.
10.

TEN TIPS FOR TIP-TOP LISTENING

Listening is both a behavior and a skill. Behavior is evidence of our ability to apply a skill. To improve our listening skills we need to consciously practice the ten tips in this section. A good driver does more than simply avoid accidents, and a good listener does more than simply pay attention.

The following tips will help you "listen louder." Consciously select those you wish to work on, then establish a list of listening priorities. The Summary Section of this book contains a Personal Action Plan. Here you will be asked to list the listening skills you want to improve, to develop some goals and to establish a plan to meet those goals.

Because business is a place where you need to listen most of the time, you will have plenty of opportunity to practice. Mentally condition yourself to make every encounter, from your first phone call to the last meeting of your business day, an opportunity to practice improved listening. Be practical and select the tips that will help you the most.

TAKE NOTES

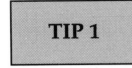

TIP 1

Good listeners are note takers. They realize that minds are imprecise and memory is imperfect. Note-taking will help you follow unorganized speakers, help you locate the key points, and identify supporting data. The following suggestions can help you improve your note-taking skills.*

Be prepared. Carry a small note pad and a pen at all times. (Some people prefer to carry a small tape recorder.) Use the pad or tape recorder regularly to record any thoughts or ideas you want to remember. Note the speaker, situation and time. (In selected situations you should ask permission before taking notes or recording what is said. Use good judgment).

Get it down. Don't take time to be overly neat. If necessary you can recopy your notes later. Write just clearly enough so you remember what you wrote and why you wrote it.

Don't try to write everything. Avoid complete sentences. Write nouns that create visual pictures. Use active verbs. Develop and use your own shorthand including symbols, pictures, punctuation and abbreviations (i.e., Suzie Hilgeman, lnch w/HP client, Fri. 11:30 @ JoJo's).

---

*For an excellent review of note-taking strategies, see *"Study Skills Strategies, Accelerate Your Learning"* in the back of the book.

LISTEN NOW, REPORT LATER

TIP 2	You can improve your listening significantly by planning to report what you heard to someone later. (Taking notes will increase your effectiveness even more.) Think of a co-worker or friend who would benefit from or enjoy the information you're listening to and plan to tell him/her what you've learned. Your listening then takes on the added dimension of a rehearsal.

CASE STUDY

Ray is the sales manager for a large manufacturing company in Seattle. Recently his company has received some customer complaints about one of their important new products. Ray quickly acted to set up a hotline and requested that all complaints be referred to him immediately.

By listening carefully to complaints from the customers, Ray was able to identify three specific manufacturing problems. He did not know personally how to solve the problems, but by responding quickly and listening carefully he assured his customers that action would be taken and the problems would be resolved. Because Ray showed concern by listening carefully, the customers agreed to support the product until a solution was found. They approved the time required to make the changes.

Ray took the information he received through listening to the manufacturing manager and carefully reported his findings. The manufacturing manager was upset by the magnitude of the problems, but he was grateful for the feedback. The manufacturing manager and his staff were able to make several adjustments to the manufacturing process which not only solved the problem, but actually improved the product.

HOW WOULD YOU RATE RAY AS A LISTENER?

_____ Excellent   _____ Good   _____ Average   _____ Fair   _____ Poor

LEARN TO WANT TO LISTEN

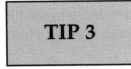

To be good listeners we must be willing to give up a preoccupation with ourselves. Simply put, we must learn to *want* to listen. The following memory device describes the skills and attitudes we need to insure our listening success:

TO BE A GOOD LISTENER, USE YOUR *DISC* DRIVE

D = Desire   From a desire to listen comes commitment. A committed athlete does not play half of each game. We must *want* to learn to listen to be effective communicators.

I = Interest   According to G. K. Chesterton, there is no such thing as an uninteresting topic, there are just uninterested people. We must learn to develop an interest in either the person and/or the topic to be good listeners.

S = Self-Discipline   We must learn self-discipline to eliminate distractions, understand the speaker's key points, overcome boredom, interpret voice inflection and tone, understand nonverbal cues and comprehend the main idea. Next time you are in a listening situation, pay attention to how well you control your listening habits. Monitoring your listening behavior is essential to taking positive action later.

C = Concentration   Concentration requires greater effort than does paying attention. You pay attention when you juggle balls, and you concentrate when you juggle eggs. Concentration is focused mental energy; and it is a limited commodity. How long can you concentrate intently in a meeting or on the telephone? Why can some people concentrate for hours, while others grow restless in minutes? Think of concentration as money in the bank. If you are like most people, your money is a limited resource. You must discipline yourself to spend it carefully. You must choose how you spend your concentration energy, as well. You will have more ability to concentrate at some times than at others. Are you more alert in the morning or the afternoon? How well do you concentrate after a heavy meal or a hard day on the job? Take advantage of your maximum ability to concentrate by:

    a) Planning your time
    b) Knowing your limits
    c) Setting listening priorities

LISTENING LAB

Complete the following exercise to identify some reasons why you do not always concentrate:

CONCENTRATION CHECKLIST

Rate the following which apply to you using a scale from 0-3, with 0 being no problem; 1 being a minor problem; 2 being somewhat of a problem; and 3 being a major problem. Total your score and compare it to the box at the end of the exercise.

---

1. I'm in a hurry ____

2. I become distracted by what is going on around me ____

3. I'm self-conscious ____

4. I'm bored ____

5. I'm thinking about what I'm going to say next ____

6. I'm in surroundings that are ''out of my comfort zone'' ____

7. I already know what the speaker is going to say ____

8. I'm used to having things repeated ____

9. I'm on mental overload most of the time ____

10. I'm not responsible for the information ____

11. I'm tired ____

12. I'm confused by the topic or the speaker ____

13. I'm daydreaming ____

0-5	You have excellent concentration skills.
6-15	This book should help improve your concentration skills.
16 or more	You need a specific action plan to improve concentration skills, and a good rest.

BE PRESENT

 TIP 3 CON'T To improve your concentration develop an opportunistic attitude. Ask yourself these questions:

- Why am I listening?

- What can I learn or pass along to a co-worker?

- How can I use this information?

Concentration improves when you develop mental pictures of what the speaker is saying. If Joe calls to say that he will have the Wilson report on your desk by 2:30 p.m. on Friday, visualize Joe placing the report on your desk. Notice how Joe is dressed. Imagine the word WILSON in bold letters on the cover of the report. See in your mind a clock that reads 2:30 p.m. next to your desk calendar turned to Friday. By visualizing what you want to remember, you create ''dwell time'' for your mind to encode the information into your long term memory.

To be a good listener, use your *DISC* Drive. Just as a disk drive runs the computer, so our personal *DISC* Drives control our attitudes, skills and behaviors in listening situations.

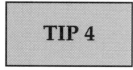 **TIP 4** Like it or not, we always choose whether and how well we are going to listen. When we choose not to listen, our minds are on vacation and we do not interpret, evaluate or respond appropriately to the speaker and the message. Only when we choose to ''be present'' are we focused on the speaker and the message.

Our number one alternative to being present is daydreaming. Daydreaming is a comfortable private escape. It normally doesn't disturb anyone and often others don't realize we're doing it. Daydreaming is what we elect to do when we choose not to be present.

Daydreaming is the single greatest barrier to active listening. To be present and listen effectively, we must recognize our mental vacations, put them aside and bring ourselves back to the subject at hand. The exercise on the facing page will help you recognize your **''DQ'' (Daydream Quotient)** and suggest steps to take to be present in your listening.

LISTENING LAB

YOUR "DQ" (DAYDREAM QUOTIENT)

In the following exercise take a piece of paper and jot down any time you daydream as you read the rest of this book. If your mind wanders, jot down where it went and what you were thinking about, then quickly return your attention to your reading. Reading and listening are similar in that they both allow opportunities for daydreaming. Notice any tendency you may have to let your mind wander as you read, and write it down. When you complete **The Business of Listening,** review your "DQ" to see if there are repeated subjects or patterns in your daydreams. If so, they may be matters for conscious attention and action.

WE ALL DAYDREAM

We all daydream; many of us as much as 50 percent of the time. Next time you are in a listening situation check your DQ to notice how often you mentally wander off while the speaker is talking. If you "wander" at least once per minute, chances are you need more concentration and self-discipline in your listening.

Effective listeners focus on the speaker and listen hard for the content of the message. They avoid the embarrassment of being caught daydreaming. While we are never tested on our daydreams, we can, at any time, be tested on the content of the message.

ANTICIPATE EXCELLENCE

TIP 5

In the film *"Brain Power"*, John Houseman presents a powerful story about a group of normal men who checked themselves into a mental hospital. Each had invented a different story explaining why he was crazy. All studied and displayed classic textbook symptoms of mental illness. Once inside the hospital they began to tell the truth, but no one believed them. Only after great difficulty and with outside verification were they released from the hospital.

Expectations play a powerful role in our lives. How often have we avoided a co-worker because we didn't want to spend time listening to small talk. Other times we may have made up an excuse to miss a speaker we expected to be boring.

By giving others a chance to speak intelligently and by anticipating excellence from them, we can help them become successful. As humans we have a deep and unending need to be heard and understood. When we set aside our needs and truly listen, people will drop their pretenses and speak to us in a more mature and connected manner. See Kathy's story on page 87.

See Kathy's story on page 87.

Listeners can help speakers by

- Asking questions
- Showing interest
- Expressing concern
- Paying attention

PEOPLE DO THEIR BEST WHEN THEY KNOW SOMEONE IS LISTENING.

THE PIONEER'S STORY

The following story is about early pioneers in covered wagons crossing into the new Oregon Territory. They stopped to rest at a small settlement and the wagon master spoke to an old man sunning himself in front of the general store.

"Say, Old Timer, what kind of people have settled out here?"

"What kind of people were they where you came from?" asked the old man.

"Well, they were mean, full of mischief and small minded. That's why we left," said the wagon master.

"Sorry to say, young feller, but that's the kind of folks you'll find out here," replied the old man.

Later in the week another team of wagons pulled into the same town for supplies. This wagon master also stopped in front of the general store and spoke to the same old man sunning on the steps.

"Say, Old Timer, what kind of people have settled out here?"

"What kind of people were they where you came from?", asked the old man again.

"The people we left behind were kind, decent people and they were generous. When we left they gave us supplies and helped us load our wagons. We all miss them very much," sighed the wagon master.

"Well, my friend, you've come to the right place, because those are the kind of people you're going to find out here," replied the old man with a kindly smile.

We get what we expect! Anticipate excellence, and it will happen a lot more often than if we assume otherwise.

BECOME A "WHOLE BODY" LISTENER

| **TIP 6** |

To be effective listeners we must involve the whole body. Not only are our ears tuned in, but so are our eyes, our minds (the intellect), our bodies, our hearts and our intuition. Good listeners give both nonverbal and verbal signals that they are listening.

A "whole body" listener tunes in by
- Conveying a positive encouraging attitude
- Sitting in an attentive posture
- Remaining alert, but comfortable
- Nodding in acknowledgment of the speaker's words
- Making good eye contact
- Listening between the lines
- Looking like a listener

If you have complete rapport you will naturally match the speaker's physical movements, tone of voice, vocabulary and breathing patterns. Good listeners are in sensory balance with the speaker.

According to Albert Mehrabian, a noted expert in human behavior, our communication is 55 percent nonverbal, 38 percent inflection and tone and only 7 percent words.

If Mehrabian is correct, then most of the message is *seen* and *sensed*, and the words are far less important than the nonverbal cues and tone of voice.

Think about your personal mannerisms and behaviors. Do you have any of the following habits that would distract or confuse a speaker?
- Fidgeting
- Blinking
- Biting your lip
- Frowning deeply
- Playing with your hair, tie or jewelry
- Looking at your watch
- Staring

Stop for a moment and think about these behaviors. Would they distract you if you were the one speaking? If your answer is yes, you need to find a way to modify your behavior. Try the suggestions on the facing page.

LISTENING LAB

1. Body Check Exercise

Briefly discuss your nonverbal listening responses with two people you know. Make one a person you enjoy and the other a person you don't. Are your responses different? If so, how? If you want to change any of your nonverbal responses to either person use the *Change* line to state your improvement goal.

Person #1 _____

| Response | Description | Change |

Posture
Eye Contact
Facial Expression
Mannerisms
General Attitude
Voice (verbal response)

Person #2 _____

| Response | Description | Change |

Posture
Eye Contact
Facial Expression
Mannerisms
General Attitude
Voice (verbal response)

2. Nonverbal Encouragement Exercise

List five things you can do nonverbally to encourage a speaker.

1.

2.

3.

4.

5.

BUILD RAPPORT BY PACING THE SPEAKER

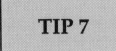

TIP 7

Pacing is a method listeners use to build a positive relationship with a speaker by imitating or mirroring his or her gestures. These gestures include: breathing, voice rate, vocabulary, favorite phrases and facial expressions. Of course, if we imitate too closely we will be accused of mimicking and our attempts to build rapport will be lost.

When pacing, the listener focuses on what the speaker is doing as well as what he or she is saying. The listener then makes a conscious effort to become more like the speaker. The speaker senses the similarities and feels at ease, because we are most comfortable with people who are more like us. When others' behaviors are very different from our own, we adjust less easily to their styles.

This technique is not meant to manipulate other people. If your intention is to build rapport, you can do it more easily if you take your attention off of yourself and focus it on the other person. That is the purpose of pacing.

As a listener, you can pace those speaking in any of the following ways:

1. **Match your voice rate to theirs.** Speed up or slow down as necessary.

2. **Change your voice volume to match theirs.**

3. **Notice and use some of the same words and phrases as the speaker.**

4. **Approximate the speaker's gestures.** Sit forward or back, hands on or off the desk, etc. (Do not be too obvious or you will be noticed. *Approximate* the gestures.)

5. **Breathe at about the same rate, without being too obvious.** (If the speaker is a Type A and breathes very fast be careful not to hyperventilate.)

CHERYL'S STORY

Cheryl was preparing to give a technical speech before a large important audience. She arrived early at the meeting room to test her slides and adapt to the circumstances of the room. When she turned on the rented projector, the bulb in the machine suddenly burned out. Cheryl looked in the projector case but could not find a replacement. Frantically she searched the building for a maintenance person. She found the maintenance supervisor on the next floor, ambling slowly down the hall. Cheryl rushed to the supervisor, explaining her dilemma in a rapid staccato voice that displayed an obvious urgency.

Bill, the supervisor was low keyed. While Cheryl churned like a buzz saw, Bill spoke no faster than a snail on Valium. Cheryl felt she could count to ten between each of Bill's words. "I'd - like - to - help - you, - but - I don't - have - a - key - to - the - supply - closet," said Bill in a low slow patient monotone. Cheryl continued to buzz and Bill continued to dawdle for another minute.

Suddenly Cheryl remembered something she had read about pacing a speaker, and she decided to give it a try. Gradually she began to slow her speech to match Bill's rate. It was painful for Cheryl to talk so slowly, but Bill became more responsive and more helpful as she became less frantic.

Within minutes Bill remembered someone who had a key, and he volunteered to find the bulb she needed. Cheryl couldn't be sure the pacing made the difference, but within fifteen minutes she had the replacement bulb. Bill flashed her a big slow smile as he handed her the bulb, along with a spare, in case the replacement burned out. Cheryl thanked him s-l-o-w-l-y, and smiled back. She had found a new friend.

BYRON'S STORY

Byron was an independent sales representative for a refrigeration company in Alaska. Because of his large territory, Byron made most of his contacts by telephone. Byron had heard of pacing from a friend and decided to try it in his cold calls and follow-up over the phone.

When he called potential customers he listened very carefully to *what* they said and *how* they said it. Then as he spoke, he paced their voices, speed, inflection and vocabulary. With no other variables in his experiment other than pacing, Byron was able to increase his refrigeration equipment sales by 30 percent over the previous quarter.

TEN TIPS FOR TIP-TOP LISTENING (continued)

$$\boxed{\text{LISTENING LAB}}$$

Pacing the Speaker

To develop an ability to pace effectively, follow these guidelines in the suggested sequence:

1. Practice pacing with a friend. Tell him or her what you are doing first. Have your friend tell you a funny story or describe an interesting place to visit and use varied gestures and facial expressions. Mirror each action and expression to get the feeling for the pacing activity. When you both stop laughing, discuss how successful you were and solicit suggestions for improvement.

2. Next, practice pacing on a friend or family member in a no-risk situation. This time try to remain undetected.

3. Finally, practice on a colleague choosing one or two characteristics to mirror. Be natural and sincere. As you pace and observe, exhibit an attitude of wanting to build rapport.

Rapport is the ultimate tool in producing positive results with others. In business, dealing effectively with people is essential. Rapport can help us achieve success. We build rapport by listening actively and acting on what we learn.

THE THREE KEYS TO PACING

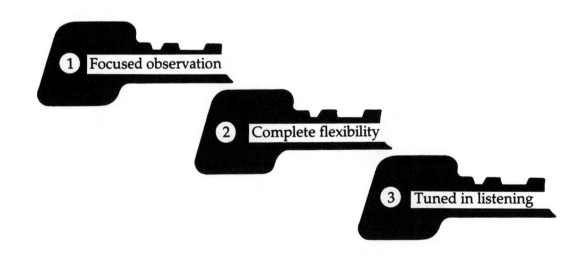

CONTROL YOUR EMOTIONAL "HOT-BUTTONS"

TIP 8	Words, issues, situations and/or personalities trigger us emotionally. When these issues trigger our emotional "hot-buttons" verbal messages become distorted, either positively or negatively. Because issues are emotional they create barriers to effective listening. When our "hot-buttons" are activated, we tune out, distort or prejudge these emotionally charged messages. The three-step method on the next page can help you identify your listening hot-buttons.

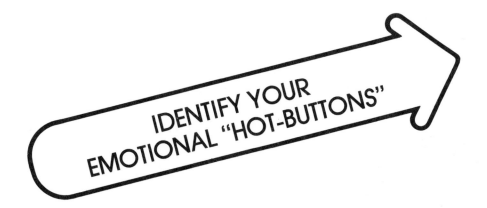

IDENTIFY YOUR EMOTIONAL "HOT-BUTTONS"

TEN TIPS FOR TIP-TOP LISTENING (continued)

| LISTENING LAB |

Identifying Emotional "Hot-buttons"

Step I   Following are some listening situations and phrases that may cause you to be emotional. Check those that are "hot-buttons" for you as a listener, and add others that strongly affect you, positively or negatively.

_____ "You never/always..."

_____ Know-it-all attitudes

_____ Individuals who smoke cigarettes or cigars while talking to you

_____ "Shut up!"

_____ Bigots

_____ Bad grammar

_____ "You never listen."

_____ Pushy individuals

_____ Whining

_____ "What you should do is..."

Others:

_____

_____

_____

Step II   Read through the list again and cross out any "hot-button" issues you are willing to give up, in other words, those you can forget, and not let them bother you any more. Chances are you will not cross off many items from your list. This step demonstrates that it is difficult to give up habitual ways of responding to emotional situations.

Step III   Check the responses on the following list that describe your physical reactions to emotionally charged issues:

        ____ Heartbeat increases.

        ____ Hands feel sweaty.

        ____ Voice shakes.

        ____ Chest tightens.

Others: ____

        ____

        ____

Emotional "hot-buttons" are intense complex feelings that affect everyone. Each may initiate a different emotional reaction, but our physical responses are similar. If you cannot eliminate your emotional "hot-buttons", the best alternative is to develop acceptable responses. The physical triggers warn you that emotions are taking over. When emotional levels go up, objectivity comes down. Problems are never satisfactorily resolved at an emotional level.

To control emotional hot-buttons we must identify what triggers us, understand our responses, and develop behaviors that allow us to listen more carefully and objectively.

TEN TIPS FOR TIP-TOP LISTENING (continued)

Ten Steps for Controlling Emotional "Hot-buttons"

Following is a list of coping skills for preventive maintenance when your hot-button is activated by someone's anger or frustration.

1. **Listen attentively without interrupting.** Take deep breaths to help you control your physical reactions.

2. **Make a *conscious* choice about your response.** You can get angry, try to solve the problem or ignore it. If you choose to solve the problem, you prevent it from happening again.

3. **Acknowledge the other person's feelings.** Make it okay for them to feel the way they do.

4. **Ask objective questions for clarification.** Open ended questions are useful.

5. **Try to see the other person's point of view.** Agree where you can and feed back what you are hearing.

6. **Stick to the subject.** Define your problem and don't let other issues interfere.

7. **Be patient.** Problems don't always have immediate solutions. Be patient with the other person—and yourself.

8. **Express your point of view.** Don't force proof. Present your evidence without backing the other person into a corner.

9. **Explain why.** A reasonable explanation can often take the sting out of an emotional issue.

10. **Work out a "win-win" plan.** Make sure your solution is fair and workable for everyone involved.

For additional suggestions refer to "The Joy of Small Change" on page 13.

LISTENING LAB

Preventive Maintenance for Emotional "Hot-buttons"

In the first column below list three people who affect you emotionally when you listen to them. Next write down the "hot-button" issue that activates your reaction. Finally, develop a preventive maintenance plan to control or modify your emotional reaction.

Person	"Hot-button"	Preventive Maintenance Plan

1.

2.

3.

CONTROL DISTRACTIONS

| TIP 9 |

Comedy star, George Carlin, once asked, ''Aren't you glad the phone wasn't invented by Alexander Graham Siren?'' A telephone is one of the biggest distractions to listening in a business environment, because unseen others choose when the phone will ring.* If the phone were the only distraction we could probably learn to tolerate it. Every day we must deal with many internal, external, visual and auditory distractions.

To be good listeners, we must control our responses to distractions or they will control us. Distractions affect the ability to listen well because of their *variety, novelty* or *intensity.* External distractions include the telephone, background noise, unfamiliarity with vocabulary, seating, lighting, etc. Internal distractions can be things such as headaches, hunger, fatigue, or a current emotional state, such as anxiety.

STEPHANIE'S STORY

Stephanie was putting the finishing touches on a major marketing project when a co-worker called to discuss a budget problem. Stephanie automatically grabbed the phone and answered while still assembling binders. Suddenly she realized her distraction and set the binders aside. She told her co-worker politely that she was just finishing a project with a tight deadline and asked if she could return the call in an hour, when the project was completed, so she could be a better listener. By handling the matter this way, Stephanie avoided being distracted. She let the caller know her desire to give the budget problem her full attention as soon as possible.

Life and work are full of distractions. Part of our professional responsibility is to manage our working environment. Although our working conditions will never be ideal, we can minimize distractions by taking action to improve our listening, which will help reduce communication failures.

*For an excellent book *Time Management on the Telephone,* see the back of the book.

LISTENING LAB

Overcoming Distractions

The following statements describe how people might handle various distractions. Check those items you do well.

☐ **Plan your listening.** Don't attempt important business in a restaurant. It's too noisy and you're interrupted frequently. Find a quiet room away from the phone for important meetings. Plan decision-making meetings during your high energy times of the day. Think about possible distractions and plan to avoid as many as you can.

☐ **Don't use distractions as a convenient excuse for not listening.** Overcome distractions with extra concentration and determination.

☐ **Identify what is causing a distraction and make adjustments.** Are you too near a noisy copier? Can you move away from it? Do you have a headache? Have you taken an aspirin? Are you hungry? Can you eat an apple? Are the lights too low or too high? Can they be adjusted? Is the phone a problem? Could someone take your calls? In other words, when you have identified the problem, you are one step closer to fixing it.

☐ **Ignore the distraction.** If you can't do anything about the distraction, tune it out by concentrating harder. Although you know the distraction is there, focus your attention on the speaker. Use self-discipline.

☐ **Call "time out" when you are too tired to listen.** Audial fatigue is caused by constant noise such as fans humming or the drone of machinery or traffic. Intense concentration or physical exhaustion can also cause "ear exhaustion." Don't be shy about calling a halt when you have had enough noise.

LISTENING IS A GIFT, GIVE GENEROUSLY

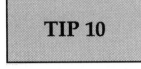

TIP 10

Listening is a skill that anyone can learn, and it is also a gift that anyone can give. It is a gift of a person's time and attention. Listening is an acknowledgment of caring. Honest listening encourages a speaker to be creative and feel more accepted.

According to author, Tom Peters, in his book, ''In Search of Excellence'' top executives have learned to be excellent listeners. They understand the importance of good listening. The best managers do far more than allow listening to happen. They realize that listening improves effectiveness, accomplishes more and earns profits.

The gift of listening assumes the speaker has value, dignity and something to offer. We must listen every day in the business world. If, in our listening, we take the focus off ourselves and encourage the speaker to express his/her ideas, we extend a gift that will be repaid many times. Develop a listening attitude. The results are worth it.

CONSIDER A GIFT CERTIFICATE

A GIFT OF LISTENING

This certificate entitles you to one-half hour of my undivided attention. I will listen to you carefully and thoughtfully. I will not interrupt, and I'll only ask questions for clarification.

When would you like your gift?

_____

Listener

P A R T

VI

SUMMARY
FIVE POINTS TO
REMEMBER

SUMMARY:
FIVE POINTS TO REMEMBER

Section I **Why Should You Listen?**

- Work and listening are inseparable.

- Lazy listening is a hidden cost in business.

- We listen for our own reasons.

- We can improve listening with desire, motivation and a plan for constructive change.

Section II **Four Key Elements of Listening: How to be a Good Listener**

- Hear the message. Listen to both verbal and nonverbal information.

- Interpret the message. A good interpretation is a match-up of meaning between the speaker and the listener.

- Evaluate the message. The listener's opinion should be based on *all* available information. Ask questions.

- Respond to the message. Good listening means giving the speaker an appropriate response, verbally and/or nonverbally.

Section III **Your Listening Style—A Barrier or a Bridge?**

- Behavior reflects attitude.

- How we look and act as listeners determines our listening style.

FIVE POINTS TO REMEMBER (continued)

Section IV   How Well Do You Listen?

- Most people aren't good listeners.

- A good listener encourages positive results.

- We listen best when there is a payoff or a penalty.

- Personal listening awareness is the key to constructive change.

Section V   Ten Tips for Tip-Top Listening

- Take notes. They aid retention.

- Listen now, report later. Plan to tell someone what you heard; you will remember it better.

- Learn to want to listen. You must have Desire, Interest, Self-discipline and Concentration to be a good listener.

- Be present. Watch the tendency to daydream.

- Anticipate excellence. We get good information more often when we expect it.

- Become a "whole-body" listener. Listen with your ears, your eyes, your heart, your intuition and your mind.

- Build rapport by pacing the speaker. Approximate the speaker's gestures, expressions and voice patterns to create comfortable communication.

- Control your emotional "hot-buttons." Knowing what makes you react emotionally is your key to preventive maintenance.

- Control distractions. Controlling internal and external distractions helps you manage your working environment more effectively.

- Give the gift of listening. Listening is a skill, and a gift. Give generously.

DEVELOP A PERSONAL ACTION PLAN

A definition of ACCOUNTABILITY is to be responsible for one's actions.

We all have good intentions. The thing that separates those who are successful from those who are not is how well these ''good intentions'' are carried out.

A voluntary action plan can convert your good intentions into actions.

The PERSONAL ACTION PLAN on the next page is a good starting point if you are serious about improving your listening skills.

This action plan can be initiated the next time you are in the role of listener.

PERSONAL ACTION PLAN

PERSONAL ACTION PLAN (continued)

Think about the information you have read in this book. Review the exercises, questionnaires and case studies. What did you learn about listening? What did you learn about yourself as a listener? How can you improve your listening skills? Make a commitment to improving your listening in your business and personal life. Design a personal action plan to help you reach your goal.

The following guide may help you clarify your goals and outline actions to achieve them.

1. My current listening skills are effective in the following areas:

2. I need to improve my listening skills in the following areas:

3. I will implement an action plan for listening improvement in the following manner:

    A. My listening goals:

    B. My *plan* for reaching my goals:

    C. My timetable:

    (Refer to page 50 ''How to Stomp Bad Habits'' for reinforcement.)

4. The following person(s) will benefit from my improved listening skills:

5. They will benefit in the following ways:

KATHY'S STORY

On Kathy Green's thirtieth birthday she cautiously invited her parents to join the celebration with a few friends. Her mother had baked Kathy's favorite lemon cake and Kathy felt obligated. However, she was concerned about what the reaction of her friends might be to her parents. Kathy's father was hard-of-hearing and shouted when he spoke. Her mother in turn shouted at her father to tell him what other people were saying. Mrs. Green also talked constantly and changed the subject frequently. Almost any response from her listener would catapult Mrs. Green onto a new topic. Kathy had long since given up really listening to her mother. Kathy's behavior was cool and polite, but non-caring.

Kathy attended a company seminar on listening shortly before the celebration. She realized that although she listened effectively to co-workers, she had developed a habitual "unhearing" response to her mother.

At her birthday dinner, Kathy began to realize that her mother's behavior was a bid for attention. Mrs. Green was isolated from her husband by his hearing loss and from her only child, by Kathy's imposed distancing. It was true that her mother did not have good communication skills, but Kathy realized that her mother changed the topic in an attempt to be more interesting. The more she was rebuffed, the more she changed the subject.

Kathy made a decision following the night of her birthday to pay more attention to her mother. She focused her listening and developed a genuine interest in what her mother was saying. She worked hard to break old listening patterns and substitute new ones. First she noticed only small changes. Her mother began to stick to the subject longer as Kathy asked patient, relevant questions and listened to the answers. At times, Kathy had to guide her mother back to the subject, but she was persistent in her resolve.

KATHY'S STORY (continued)

After six months Kathy noticed that her mother was calmer and more connected when she spoke. She stopped talking as much and listened with interest as Kathy told her about a recent promotion. True, Mrs. Green still shouted at Mr. Green, but Kathy stopped hearing it as much. Thanks to a simple increase in listening effectiveness, Kathy was able to renew a loving relationship with her parents.

Kathy learned well the business of listening and we hope you are on your way to doing the same. Good Luck!

FOR OTHER FIFTY-MINUTE SELF-STUDY BOOKS
SEE THE BACK OF THIS BOOK.

FOR OTHER FIFTY-MINUTE SELF-STUDY BOOKS
SEE THE BACK OF THIS BOOK.

NOTES

FOR OTHER FIFTY-MINUTE SELF-STUDY BOOKS
SEE THE BACK OF THIS BOOK.

OVER 150 BOOKS AND 35 VIDEOS AVAILABLE IN THE 50-MINUTE SERIES

We hope you enjoyed this book. If so, we have good news for you. This title is part of the best-selling *50-MINUTE*™ *Series* of books. All *Series* books are similar in size and identical in price. Many are supported with training videos.

To order *50-MINUTE* Books and Videos or request a free catalog, contact your local distributor or Crisp Publications, Inc., 1200 Hamilton Court, Menlo Park, CA 94025. Our toll-free number is (800) 442-7477.

50-Minute Series Books and Videos Subject Areas . . .

Management
Training
Human Resources
Customer Service and Sales Training
Communications
Small Business and Financial Planning
Creativity
Personal Development
Wellness
Adult Literacy and Learning
Career, Retirement and Life Planning

Other titles available from Crisp Publications in these categories

Crisp Computer Series
The Crisp Small Business & Entrepreneurship Series
Quick Read Series
Management
Personal Development
Retirement Planning